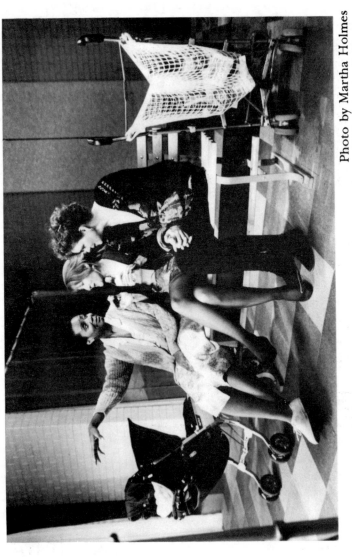

Photo by Martha Holmes

Tonya Pinkins, Mia Dillon and Dierdra O'Connell in a scene from The Woman's Project production of "Approximating Mother." Set design by David Jenkins.

APPROXIMATING MOTHER

BY KATHLEEN TOLAN

★

★

DRAMATISTS
PLAY SERVICE
INC.

APPROXIMATING MOTHER premiered at The Women's Project (Julia Miles, Artistic Director), in New York City, on October 29, 1991. It was directed by Gloria Muzio; the set design was by David Jenkins; the costume design was by Elsa Ward; the lighting design was by Jackie Manassee; the sound design was by Mark Bennett and the production stage manager was Judy Dennis. The cast was as follows:

MOLLY	Mia Dillon
BRENA	Shawana Kemp
FRAN	Deirdre O'Connell
ELLIE, SYLVIA, GRACE	Tonya Pinkins
JACK, EUGENE	Richard Poe
MAC	Steven Ryan
JEN	Ali Thomas

CHARACTERS

MOLLY
FRAN, Molly's best friend
JACK, Molly's husband
ELLIE, the midwife
MAC SULLIVAN, a lawyer
JEN
SYLVIA, a social worker
EUGENE, Jen's father
BRENA, Jen's friend
GRACE, a nanny

Seven actors could do this, with an actor playing Eugene and Jack, and an actor playing Ellie and Sylvia and Grace.

SETTING

The action takes place in New York City, now, and, in the scenes with Jen, somewhere in Indiana.

APPROXIMATING MOTHER

SCENE ONE

A Japanese restaurant. Molly sits at a table, thinking. She is very pregnant. Fran's coat is draped over the opposite chair. Now Fran comes in and joins Molly.

FRAN.   No message. He's not interested. I have to face it. The first relatively interesting male I've encountered in I'd say about a year and a half — if I get to count Peter —

MOLLY.   He really can't be counted. He was *not* available for the long —

FRAN.   Yes but —

MOLLY.   And he wouldn't let you *say* anything during sex.

FRAN.   Did I tell you that?

MOLLY.   Yes.

FRAN.   But he *was* interesting. Face it.

MOLLY.   Yes but he still doesn't count.

FRAN.   Then it's been like five years.

MOLLY.   Evan was the last.

FRAN.   Dear Evan. Why did I...?

MOLLY.   That's what you say now. You were miserable. He only cared about you when you'd decided to leave him.

FRAN.   True. Then why do we get to count him?

MOLLY.   Well. You were with him six years.

FRAN.   True.

MOLLY.   But why have we written off this guy Ted? Just because he hasn't called —

FRAN.   Molly. He said he'd call me the next day. It's been two weeks.

MOLLY.   Maybe he's gone out of town. Isn't he a journalist or something? Maybe he had a hot tip.

FRAN.   Right. Head for the hills and don't look back. I checked with his service. He's in town.

MOLLY.   Oh.

FRAN.   I knew it anyway. These fucking cowards. I knew it at the time. It's just that he'd actually brought me *flowers* and a box of *candy*. I mean, he was really, you know, paying *attention*.

MOLLY.   Uh huh.

FRAN.   It was so ... *heterosexual,* so old *fashioned.*

MOLLY.   Yeah.

FRAN.   And he didn't spend all of dinner talking about his mother like that guy Francis did.

MOLLY.   Right.

FRAN.   Nor did he do an hour on his body building technique.

MOLLY.   Uh huh.

FRAN.   Though he didn't ask me a single question about myself. Talked non-stop about himself, his work, his perceptions of various things, but it was interesting and I thought maybe he was nervous, as I was. All I did was nod and smile, really. He must have thought I'd recently had a lobotomy or something.

MOLLY.   Oh, Fran.

FRAN.   He did tell me this story about how his best friend who's this very eccentric, unconventional, brilliant Parisian woman writer-journalist —

MOLLY.   How nice.

FRAN.   They were in a restaurant and she was served an omelette and called the waitress back and said it was rubbery and the waitress said it was the best they could do and she picked it up and slapped it against the wall and said "I didn't order a fly swatter." And I guess he's telling me this story so I know who his model is and isn't it fantastic to be so witty and irreverent and I just nod and smile dully and feel incredibly old and tired.

MOLLY.   Yes.

FRAN.   Anyway, we went back to my apartment, had some more wine and I decided I needed to make more of an effort. This is really embarrassing. I pulled out my violin.

MOLLY.   Why is this embarrassing? What did you do with it?

FRAN.   Molly. I played it. I hadn't played it since *high school* when I decided the best and most effective revenge on my mother was to quit playing the violin. It was awful. There I was, the performing seal, playing Paganini *terribly*.

MOLLY.   You really like him.

FRAN.   Then I showed him my scrapbooks.

MOLLY.   Really?

FRAN.   Then when he said good night — I know this is shocking, but I had known him, you know, peripherally, for years —

MOLLY.   You slept with him.

FRAN.   I just took him and gave him this long kiss and we ended up in bed and it was nice but I thought as he responded to my initial embrace, "He obliges."

MOLLY.   Oh, god.

FRAN.   He was *obliging* me.

MOLLY.   Right.

FRAN.   Very polite.

MOLLY.   Uh huh.

FRAN.   But it had nothing to do with whatever his own impulse might've been.

MOLLY.   Right.

FRAN.   The whole thing was, let's face it, humiliating.

MOLLY.   Right. *(Pause.)*

FRAN.   Anyway, the next day I took him up to Esther and Phil's and we all hung around with the baby.

MOLLY.   Are you serious?

FRAN.   And, yes, it's true, I thought it was a good test. I really don't want to waste time on these guys who don't want families.

MOLLY.   But — they really are, so often, cowards, you know, you can't just —

FRAN.   I know, I know, but I'm really sick of it. I just plopped the baby into his lap and I saw this like veil drop

7

over his cool blue eyes as he smiled this slightly frozen smile and then made all the appropriate coos and continued to be quite charming but I knew that was it. I'd done it. *(Pause. Molly watches Fran eat her sushi.)*

MOLLY.   God, that looks good.

FRAN.   Help yourself.

MOLLY.   I can't. It has little bugs in it or something that could make Bob sick.

FRAN.   Bob?

MOLLY.   Oh. Jane said, "When the baby pops out of your tummy and the doctor catches it, I will call her Bob."

FRAN.   Great.

MOLLY.   First thing I'm going to have, sushi and Jack Daniels.

FRAN.   Mmm. I'll buy.

MOLLY.   You're on. *(Beat.)* Janey asked me last week how I got pregnant.

FRAN.   And...?

MOLLY.   I say the stuff about having an egg ...

FRAN.   Uh huh.

MOLLY.   She wants to know if I eat an egg.

FRAN.   Oh.

MOLLY.   I say no, inside my body, and Daddy planted the seed.

FRAN.   Right.

MOLLY.   She wants to know if the seed was from the garden, I say no, then I'd've had a carrot! We laugh. So she asks where he planted it, I say in my vagina. She says, Oh. Two days later. We're walking home from school, and she says, did Daddy plant the seed with his hand?

FRAN.   Oh oh.

MOLLY.   And I say, no, it came from his body, out of his penis. She says, oh. Two days later, she says, but, that seed of Daddy's — did it just fly across the air into your vagina?

FRAN.   How sweet.

MOLLY.   So I have to break it to her, and she says, absolutely horrified, "He put his *penis inside* your *vagina*? Are you *serious?* "And then she asks if it tickled a little bit. I say yes,

8

a little bit. And she laughs and says that's really strange and that's it.

FRAN.   God. *(Pause.)* You don't want me there, let's face it.

MOLLY.   Where? Face what? Yes I do. What are you talking about?

FRAN.   Bob's birth.

MOLLY.   You're chickening out.

FRAN.   You have a husband! He doesn't want me there.

MOLLY.   He loves you.

FRAN.   But it's your special thing.

MOLLY.   He was delighted you were going to be there. It'll let him off the hook. He was terrible when Janey was born, completely frantic, hit an intern, threw up on the floor, they had to take him out. Don't you remember?

FRAN.   Yes.

MOLLY.   He told me the other night I never loved him.

FRAN.   What?!

MOLLY.   I was telling him how Jimmy had told me *he* feels like *Doreen* doesn't really love *him*, they never, like, spontaneously hop into bed, it always has to be planned, and he doesn't feel she's reacting to *him, exactly,* and Jack says, well, that's how I feel about you. I've never felt you really love me. And I say, what are you talking about? How could you feel this? You've always felt this and never told me? You've just been living this lie, sleeping beside me every night? And I just lose it. And he calls me a lunatic, says only *I* am so convoluted that I would consider *me* not loving *him his* betrayal. Which in a way makes sense I guess but at the time I felt, christ, I couldn't sleep beside him for one night much less six years thinking he didn't really love me and didn't he care?

FRAN.   Jesus. Why do I want to get married? That's the real mystery.

MOLLY.   So I'm completely hysterical. And he says, see, someone else would've said something reassuring like of course I love you, but *you* — it's all about *you,* isn't it. Methinks thou doth protest too much. And I really think he's driving me crazy. I thought he hadn't been making love to me because he's a fattist which is kind of despicable if you

9

focus on it but most people are that way and really if you focus on every little thing you really will just stop.

FRAN.   *(Thinking about herself.)* Right.

MOLLY.   Just stop.

FRAN.   Yeah.

MOLLY.   So I thought, don't get upset about it, it'll pass, this is just a temporary condition, of course wishing he was one of those guys who was completely into the whole thing, you know? Who get completely turned on by their wive's ripening, marvel at the miracle —

FRAN.   Good luck.

MOLLY.   Right. Anyway, I just couldn't get up the next morning. Jack got up with Jane who had a fit, came sobbing into the bedroom begging me to get up but I just couldn't and she refused to go to school and Jack got the babysitter to come and I just lay in bed crying all day. Finally, Irene had to leave so I got up and went in and lay on the couch and Jane gave me this really strange look and I said, "I was sick. But now I'm better." And she smiled this kind of fake smile and said, "Oh." And I said, "Were you worried about me?" And she said, "Yes. I thought you were going to die of sadness."

End Scene

SCENE TWO

Molly, Jack, Fran and Ellie the midwife are in the birthing room. Molly is in the last stages of labor. She huffs and groans, pacing back and forth, stopping to lean against a chair from time to time. Jack sits in a rocking chair, next to the birthing bed, reading aloud from War And Peace. *Ellie sits in a chair on the other side of the bed. She is reading a dog magazine. Fran stands, leaning against the wall for support or clutching a chair.*

JACK. " 'Impossible!' said Prince Andrey. 'That would be too base.' 'Time will show,' said Bilibin, letting the creases run off his forehead again in token of being done with the subject."

MOLLY. Oh, Jesus. Fuck.

FRAN. *(Herself about to faint.)* Molly?

JACK. "When Prince Andrey went to the room that had been prepared for him, and lay down in the clean linen on the feather-bed and warmed and fragrant pillows, he felt as though the battle of which he brought tidings was far, far away from him." *(Molly is moaning, groaning. Ellie gets up, goes to Molly, holds her, does the rhythmic breathing, blowing out in three short breaths and then one long, until Molly joins her.)*

ELLIE. Want some ice chips? *(Molly nods. Ellie goes out.)*

JACK. "The Prussian Alliance, the treachery of Austria, the new triumph of Bonaparte, the levee and parade and the audience of Emperor Francis next day, engrossed his attention."

MOLLY. Jack.

JACK. Yeah?

MOLLY. Stop.

JACK. The reading? It's enough?

MOLLY. Yeah.

JACK. Okay. *(Ellie comes in with a cup of ice chips.)*

ELLIE. Here we go. *(Ellie gives Molly the ice, goes back to her chair, picks up the magazine.)*

FRAN. *(Weakly.)* Molly, is there anything I can do?

MOLLY. No, Fran, it's okay.

ELLIE. *(To Jack.)* Do you guys have a dog?

JACK. No. We did have. Actually, Nickel was killed in traffic.

ELLIE. Really?

JACK. It was very sad.

ELLIE. You've got to keep them on a leash.

JACK. Yeah. *(Molly moans, grunts.)*

MOLLY. Fuck.

JACK. Then we got Lucy. But it turned out she hated kids. So when Molly got pregnant with Jane we gave her away.

ELLIE. Uh huh. We have the most wonderful airedale. They

are absolutely fabulous dogs. Very smart, very friendly, don't shed — great for allergies — *(Ellie jumps up, goes to Molly.)*

MOLLY. Oh, god.

ELLIE. Let's see how you're doing. *(Ellie guides her over to the bed, Molly's bent over, resists getting in. Jack gets up to help.)*

FRAN. *(Weak.)* You're doing great, Moll. Jesus.

ELLIE. Atta girl. Let's get you up — up on to the bed. *(Molly continues to groan, shriek, pant. She leans against the bed. Firm.)* Upsie daisy. Come on. I need to see what's happening. Come on, Molly.

JACK. Come on, honey. *(Molly manages to get up and onto her back. Ellie listens to Molly's abdomen with a stethoscope. Jack holds her hand.)*

ELLIE. Okay. Let's get her out.

MOLLY. Can I push?

ELLIE. Go. *(Molly pushes.)*

FRAN. Oh, Moll. Oh, honey. Oh my god. God.

ELLIE. Good. Hold on. Hold on. Okay. Push. *(Molly pushes.)*

JACK. Here she comes. Oh, my god.

FRAN. I can't believe it.

ELLIE. Good. Good girl. *(Ellie catches the baby, puts it on Molly's stomach.)*

MOLLY. Oh, my god.

JACK. Oh. Look at her.

FRAN. It's a girl. It's a miracle. I feel sick. *(Fran goes to a chair, sits.)*

MOLLY. Hello. Hello, sweetheart.

JACK. She's so sweet.

MOLLY. She's a little fish.

JACK. She is a little fish.

MOLLY. Oh, god, what a relief.

End Scene

SCENE THREE

Jack and Fran in the hospital cafeteria, at a table, sipping tea.

JACK. You know, it isn't so simple, to stand on the outside and watch something so, so primitive, so profound. All these months, watching her get bigger, and myself not feeling ... comfortable about it. That sounds absurd. It's just, you know, if you want some supper, you can just order it. You don't need to go wring the chicken's neck, pluck it, drain it, singe it, whatever one does to chickens, cook it. And so on — nature — and the time things naturally take — it's all so divorced from one's life these days. I mean, it really did seem incredible to me that, once we decided to have a baby — this happened with Janey and again now with whatever her name will be — got any ideas?

FRAN. Um ...

JACK. She had an amnio, we could've known it was going to be a girl, we'd've had all this time to think of a name. The doctor knew. There it was, in her file, maybe it was the fear of getting too attached, if it didn't work out. And Molly felt it took the mystery out of it, although I must say I think there's plenty of mystery left.

FRAN. Right.

JACK. But — it did seem incredible to me that we couldn't just order it. That it really would take nine months and that Molly would have to go through the whole, you know, physical experience.

FRAN. Yes.

JACK. That we are, still, in the hands of nature. It really is quite — incredible.

FRAN. Yes.

JACK. And ... to see her in such pain and not be able to do anything. Not being a woman, feeling on the outside, maybe threatened in some way. Feeling very ... male.

FRAN. Yes. *(Fran, her head on her hand, begins to fall asleep.)*

13

JACK.   And, of course, we men.... There are all those clas-
sic fears, if you subscribe to that ... of disappearing into her,
of all her secretions, of blood, of milk, how foreign her body
is. And the fear that she doesn't really love me, is just using
me. The ease and intimacy she has with other women, and
with our daughter. When I speak to Janey I always see the
quotation marks.

End Scene

SCENE FOUR

Hospital room. Molly in bed. Fran holding the baby.

FRAN.   *(Moved, tender.)* Oh, Moll.
MOLLY.   Sweet, huh?
FRAN.   God. And she's all here?
MOLLY.   Um.
FRAN.   All the fingers and toes?
MOLLY.   Oh. I guess so.
FRAN.   *(Incredulous.)* You haven't checked?
MOLLY.   No.
FRAN.   Incredible. You're so ... stable. It's the first thing I'd
do. I'd be terrified I'd had a frog.
MOLLY.   Huh. Well ... I guess I'd've noticed. *(Beat.)* Why
don't you check? *(Fran unwraps infant, counts fingers and toes.)*
FRAN.   All here. *(Beat, then she blurts out.)* I'm sorry.
MOLLY.   What?
FRAN.   I failed you.
MOLLY.   What are you talking about?
FRAN.   What's the point of having a friend if she's going
to feel threatened, thrown, overwhelmed, frozen at the sight
of her best friend's pain, panicked at the — the — physical-
ity, the biology of it all.
MOLLY.   *(Laughs.)* You were fine. I was glad you were there.
FRAN.   *(She focusses on the baby.)* God. You realize she's no

14

heavier than a bag of sugar? You go to the grocery store and get a five pound bag of sugar and this is what it weighs. This whole human.

MOLLY.   Yeah.

FRAN.   *(To baby..)* Can you say, "Fran?" Say, "Hi, Fran, you're looking gorgeous, I wish I could go home with *you* — my mommy already has a kid — she'll be too distracted, exhausted, I won't get enough attention —"

MOLLY.   How was your date last night?

FRAN.   You don't want to know.

MOLLY.   Yes I do.

FRAN.   We ate, went back to his apartment, kissed, he fell asleep, right there in the chair, I'm sitting there wondering what to do next, and he wakes up and tells me he's just dreamed that he and I were lying side by side and suddenly he realized a scorpion was crawling up his leg.

MOLLY.   Good god.

FRAN.   I left.

MOLLY.   Jesus.

FRAN.   *(After a beat.)* Molly, I'm not waiting to get the guy. I'm going to have a kid.

MOLLY.   What do you mean?

FRAN.   I'm too desperate. I'll just get married to get to be a mother and it won't be fair to the guy or the kid or me and anyway it's just too difficult, I really do feel too desperate.

MOLLY.   But — how will you do it?

FRAN.   You think it's a terrible idea.

MOLLY.   No.

FRAN.   Just because you have this ideal life doesn't mean that the rest of us can't — aspire to something.

MOLLY.   I don't have an ideal life. We're always fighting. We're completely broke. We can't pay our taxes. They just put a lien on our bank account.

FRAN.   *(Devastated.)* Molly, why didn't you tell me?

MOLLY.   It happened last week. I've been busy. It's just that, you know, lives can seem quite ideal, from the outside.

FRAN.   But I thought I was on the inside.

MOLLY. You are. *(Beat.)*

FRAN. What are you going to do?

MOLLY. I got a call from Babs Silverman — remember her?

FRAN. Sort of.

MOLLY. She said there was an opening in the art department where she is in South Carolina.

FRAN. What a terrible idea.

MOLLY. Jack says he'll die if he has to leave New York. There are no newsstands outside of New York. I said, subscribe. But he feels he has to be able to walk into a newsstand and be surrounded by three hundred publications from all over the world, it gives him this necessary energy or something. That and the Mets.

FRAN. The Mets are in terrible shape.

MOLLY. That's what I said.

FRAN. I don't want you to go. Who will I have to pick on?

MOLLY. True. *(Beat.)* So. How're you going to do it?

FRAN. Oh. I thought about just getting laid or artificially inseminated or adopt. I'll probably adopt. I mean, no offense but if you can avoid the extreme conditions —

MOLLY. They do get pretty extreme.

FRAN. So I'll get a kid and then I won't feel so desperate anymore and the right guy will come along and I won't scare him away because I'll already have my kid and I'll just be like most thirty-eight-year-old women who are divorced with a kid and we'll fall in love and it'll be fabulous.

MOLLY. I answered the phone this morning and this little voice said "Hi, Mommy." I didn't recognize her. I'd never talked to her on the phone, never heard her voice isolated from the rest of her. She sounded like any little kid. Tears started streaming down my face. She said she missed me, I said I missed her, she told me what had happened since she'd gotten up. They'd spilled the box of Cheerios on the rug. Daddy'd called our downstairs neighbor and he brought his dog up to clean up the Cheerios. She has a cold so they won't let her visit. I hung up and felt so far away.

End Scene

SCENE FIVE

Mac Sullivan's office. Mac sits behind his desk listening to Fran who sits across from him.

FRAN.   I haven't wanted, in my life, to compromise.
MAC.   Right.
FRAN.   I mean, when it really mattered to me.
MAC.   Uh huh.
FRAN.   I don't claim to be, you know, Joan of Arc —
MAC.   Right.
FRAN.   — but, you know, a lot of my friends, because they wanted to go somewhere, get somewhere, you know, have a certain amount of success, um, are doing things, representing things or, um, philosophies, ideas, they never would have ...
MAC.   Right.
FRAN.   And there's been, often, the question of how to support the children —
MAC.   Ah ha! Idealism fades in the grim light of economic reality. The excruciating journey to maturity.
FRAN.   Yes. Yes. And the question, too, "Am I really willing, at age forty, to live in quite the austerity I embraced in my twenties."
MAC.   We're not Gandhi.
FRAN.   Yes. And as a woman, you know, you hold out for as long as you can for the man who will really — I mean, *really* think of you as a, like, actual person, autonomous, with *really* as much of a right to a whole life.
MAC.   Huh.
FRAN.   I mean, I think there are men who are now able to think of a woman as separate but equal as a colleague but not as a wife.
MAC.   Huh.
FRAN.   Obviously there are exceptions and I haven't read a study or anything but it is my feeling.
MAC.   Uh huh.

17

FRAN.   Anyway — sorry — I am getting to the   — this is leading somewhere. I just never felt I *really* would be able to, you know, not be "the wife," however "modern" he might seem. With every — not that there were so many — serious relationship, I felt, however unconsciously, that I should be serving him. Or that — that I couldn't — couldn't *really* have my own thoughts. My own private thoughts. Anyway, not pretending to be, you know, a moral arbiter, just trying to retain my integrity. Certainly I'm sophisticated enough to know one's own neuroses are always tied up in — in fact, often *inform*, if not *determine*, one's philosophy, one's actions. Um. *(Pause.)* Anyway, with all of this, finally feeling very, sort of, lonely and, you know, "Is this it?"

MAC.   Right.

FRAN.   And then beginning to think about a baby. Wanting that, the feeling, the sensuality —

MAC.   Uh huh.

FRAN.   — the basicness of, you know, the tasks.

MAC.   Uh huh.

FRAN.   And the clarity of one's priorities, one's own reason for, you know, carrying on.

MAC.   Right.

FRAN.   And of course, they're so sweet.

MAC.   There's nothing sweeter.

FRAN.   And I imagine I would feel more ... connected to, you know, life, to the cycle, to the world, to humanity.

MAC.   Right.

FRAN.   And, I guess, it seems *manageable.* I mean, so much in the world seems so overwhelming, so impossible. This would be a life I might actually have some effect on. Not that I would — I mean, I'd try to honor her or him, to help and guide but not to impose my own ...

MAC.   Uh huh.

FRAN.   And, I guess, to feel connected to the — the awe — to the mystery — I don't mean the mystery of birth and life, though, of course, but, I see it with my friends, that the most basic, most boring — to the outsider — achievements of their young children are absolutely thrilling. It's as if they themselves are children again, are experiencing the miracle of — of how the world works and what it is to be alive. And, of course the problems that arise can be quite daunting, but, again, the scale seems ... manageable.

MAC. Uh huh. *(She's finished. She waits for his response. He studies her.)* Well. It isn't easy.

FRAN. Yes.

MAC. Hardest thing I've ever done, raise kids. And my wife gets the credit. I last about two hours before I'm ready to chuck 'em all — or myself — out the window. I have no patience for that day to day nagging, fighting, entertaining, ga ga go go shit. Sorry.

FRAN. Yes.

MAC. Then there's the mothers with the careers who stick the kids with the nannies twelve hours a day. I'm not talking working class who maybe have no choice. I'm talking very simple motivation: selfishness, greed. You follow? Why do they have kids? For their own occasional comfort, they feel more complete, they're more socially acceptable in the community.

FRAN. I'm lucky to have work that I can do at home.

MAC. Uh huh. Well, I don't know, manageable. Compromise. Holding out for a guy who's going to think of you as a whole person.

FRAN. Yes.

MAC. You think men don't wish for the same thing? You think we're not diminished, reduced to what she wants from me, expects of me, blames me for?

FRAN. Oh.

MAC. So the freedom is lost. The more idiosyncratic quirks are pushed underground. What you don't share is lost. You follow?

FRAN. Yes.

MAC. I don't know. *(Beat. Then he looks through his papers.)* Whatta we got here? Let's see. Depends on what you can afford. Let's see. Due date March twenty second. Pre-pregnancy weight one twenty five, Baptist — *(Checks another paper.)* what'd you say you? — Catholic.

FRAN. Yes.

MAC.   Practicing?

FRAN.   No. But I could.

MAC.   Uh huh. *(Back to papers.)* Never used drugs, cheerleader in high school, has two years of college, a time buyer for an ad agency.

FRAN.   Why isn't she keeping the child?

MAC.   Why isn't she keeping the child. Good question. Here you are, desperate for a baby, right? It's a mystery. I mean, why do women have abortions? The man split, you can't afford it, it isn't convenient, it pulls you out of the competition with the guys at the firm, you want to stay a kid. There are a thousand reasons.

FRAN.   Uh huh.

MAC.   This one's very desirable. Let's see. It would be, roughly, twenty thou.

FRAN.   Oh ...

MAC.   All inclusive. We cover the birth, hospital expences, support her for the last three months, legal fees, Indiana court fees.

FRAN.   *(Thrown.)* I ... I don't think I have that.

MAC.   You don't think you have that.

FRAN.   *(Trying to get her bearings.)* I'm sorry.

MAC.   What do you think you have?

FRAN.   I don't know.

MAC.   You don't know. *(Considers her. Beat.)* I don't know. Who knows? *(Beat.)* It's a big decision. You think I don't wonder, what would it be like if carrying my family on my back like Sisyphus weren't the *center*, the main event of my life. I remember how it was, in law school, the freedom, the possibility. The law, argument. Concepts of justice.

FRAN.   Yes.

MAC.   I'll be honest. I look at these gays, I think, lucky bastard, he doesn't have to work like a slave, come home every day to the constant demands.

FRAN.   Yes. *(Beat.)*

MAC.   What about a father?

FRAN.   Yes.

MAC.   You know, babies are in great demand. People are

desperate for babies. White — if you'll let me speak frankly —

FRAN.   Yes.

MAC.   — healthy babies. I could get one for you. I could pick up the phone right now and arrange it. *(Looks through papers.)* Here's something. One night stand. Not sure she's going to give it up. If she does, expences'll be less. Could maybe get it for twelve thou. Want to try for that?

FRAN.   I don't know. I think so. Yes.

MAC.   Now that's decisive. Just kidding. It's not simple. *(Beat.)* Why do I have kids? Convention. Obligation. Love. A wish for ownership. Control. To have made something in my own image. To continue the race, follow God's wish.

FRAN.   Yes.

MAC.   Would you like to have a drink with me later?

FRAN.   No. Thank you.

MAC.   No harm in trying.

FRAN.   Of course.

MAC.   You're very beautiful.

FRAN.   Thank you.

MAC.   Very proud.

FRAN.   Yes.

MAC.   And honest.

FRAN.   Yes.

MAC.   I like that.

FRAN.   Good.

MAC.   We'll find you something, okay?

FRAN.   Okay.

End Scene

SCENE SIX

Jen and Sylvia sit in Sylvia's office. Jen is about six months pregnant.

JEN.   I didn't used anything.
SYLVIA.   Uh huh.
JEN.   Didn't think we'd do it.
SYLVIA.   Right.
JEN.   And I thought about it a lot while we were doing it, thought I should say something but I guess I felt shy so I kept putting it off. And then I thought, well, he won't go all the way without asking if I'm on the pill or getting some rubbers or something. And then he was inside me and I kept putting it off and didn't want to interrupt and then he came inside me and I thought, "shit." But then I thought, well, I'm not so regular anyway, so who knows when I'm going to be ovulating. Think of all the times I *haven't* done it this month. The odds are really good I was ovulating one of those times.
SYLVIA.   Hmm.
JEN.   So when my period was late, I thought, "Shit —"
SYLVIA.   Hm.
JEN.   — but then, well, it's been late before and I just tried not to think about it. And I started feeling really bloated and my breasts started getting really tender and big but I really just tried not to think about it. Finally I couldn't zip my jeans and I faced the fact I had to do something so I called my girlfriend Brena and she helped me find a clinic and we went to the doctor and he said I was pregnant and I said I wanted an abortion and he said I had to have permission from my parents and I said I didn't want to tell them and he told me I should go to this social worker woman —
SYLVIA.   Who was that?
JEN.   Um. Her name was Mrs. Nelson.
SYLVIA.   What agency?
JEN.   Um. I don't know. He just gave me her number.
SYLVIA.   Uh huh.

JEN.   And said she'd help me and wouldn't tell my parents
so I went to her and she told me I would regret it if I had
an abortion, and I said I regretted this whole thing but that's
what I wanted to do and I didn't want to have a baby, I
wanted to finish high school and stuff, and she said if I wasn't
ready to be a mother there were many wonderful couples who
would love a baby and I said, well that's fine but I don't want
to do that, so she said I needed to have permission from my
parents and then I should come back to her and she'd help
me but I should think about how I'd feel if my parents had
decided not to have me and I said, "Huh?" And she said she
knew this must be a very scary and confusing time for me
and I should know she was my friend and I said I didn't
think so and then she got really nasty because she knew I
could see right through her and she started screeching, "Go
ahead, kill the baby. Kill the baby. See how it makes you
feel." And some day I'd wish I had a baby, wouldn't I, and I
said I don't know what you're talking about, let me out of
here and went home and went up to my room and was just
shaking and crying and I told my mom I had the flu and just
stayed up there for a couple of days and finally I told my
mom I was pregnant. And then everybody completely freaked
out and here I am.
SYLVIA.   Good. Good. You glad you can get this out?
JEN.   *(Hesitant.)* Yeah.
SYLVIA.   Good. I'm glad you're here. *(Pause. Jen shifts in her
chair.)* And now you say you want to keep the baby.
JEN.   Yeah.
SYLVIA.   What made you decide that?
JEN.   Um. Well, they wouldn't give me permission to have
an abortion and here I am stuck with it. I mean, I know I
could give it up but I don't want to do that. That'd be really
... I don't know. I don't want to do that.
SYLVIA.   Mm hm.
JEN.   And anyway, here I am and I can't go back home —
SYLVIA.   They want you to come back. As soon as the baby
is born. They just can't handle the baby.
JEN.   Yeah, well, that's just ... I don't want to.

SYLVIA.   Uh huh. It's a tough decision.

JEN.   Uh huh.

SYLVIA.   So let's ask the tough questions, okay?

JEN.   Okay.

SYLVIA.   Whose gonna pay the medical bills?

JEN.   I don't know.

SYLVIA.   Your parents gonna pay them?

JEN.   No.

SYLVIA.   No insurance, right?

JEN.   I don't know.

SYLVIA.   The father's not going to pay. You got a friend maybe with some money?

JEN.   No.

SYLVIA.   Okay. Let's just skip that one for now. Let's say you get out of the hospital. How you gonna support yourself and the baby?

JEN.   I'll get a job.

SYLVIA.   Okay. And who's gonna take care of the baby?

JEN.   I don't know. I'll get a babysitter.

SYLVIA.   Okay. *(Beat.)* I've seen a lot of girls go through this place. Some of them choose to give their babies up for adoption, go back home, finish high school, get training, or even go on to college, eventually get married and have a family. The ones who keep the children. *(Beat.)* It's a hard road. Most cases, the father's long gone, they end up on welfare or doing some lousy job while their kids are in some kind of nightmare childcare situation and there's no way out. *(Beat.)* You know how it feels to work all day at a job you hate, come home, to a screaming baby? Never go out, never get a break. *(Beat.)* You know that most abusive mothers started to have kids when they were teenagers? They beat their kids. Because teenagers are bad? No way. It's hard. They're frustrated. They lash out. But they're ruining more than their own lives, understand?

JEN.   I heard the heart beat. I hadn't been thinking of it being, you know, alive. And the doctor let me listen and I heard this thump, thump, thump ... I couldn't believe it. And it's starting to move around ...

SYLVIA.   Uh huh. Well. Just think about it. I know you'll make the right decision, okay?

End Scene

SCENE SEVEN

Molly and Fran sit on a bench in Washington Square playground. Molly's baby is asleep in her Snugli.

MOLLY.   The other night, I'm nursing Baby Girl —
FRAN.   I thought you'd decided on Priscilla.
MOLLY.   Jack remembered he had an aunt named Priscilla he didn't like. We just can't agree on one. The birth certificate people finally just put Baby Girl. Janey's calling her Bob. Maybe if I could have just one night of uninterrupted sleep my brain would come back.
FRAN.   Poor Molly.
MOLLY.   So I'm nursing the baby while getting a bath ready for Janey —
FRAN.   Jesus.
MOLLY.   And I'm weak with hunger and exhausted and tense and just thinking, one more hour, they'll be in bed, I'll put my feet up, relax, eat, if I can just make it through one hour — where is she? *(They rise, look for Janey.)*
FRAN.   On the slide.
MOLLY.   Right. *(They both wave to Janey, then sit.)* So I'm helping Janey out of her dress and she throws it on the floor and I say, very civil, very restrained, "Honey, would you please take your dress into your room?" and she says, "No." And I think, oh, oh, this could be the straw. But I cling to my calm veneer and say, "Please, dear, don't just throw your dress on the floor. Put it on your bed and I'll hang it up later." And she says, "No. I don't have to." And I lose it. "Okay, that's *it,*" I say, "You're driving me *fucking crazy.*"
FRAN.   Oh, dear.

MOLLY.   And she bursts into tears and says, "But I'm a kid. Kids shouldn't have to do these things." And I say, "I've got to get out of here" —

FRAN.   Incredible.

MOLLY.   And Janey's sobbing, clinging to my skirt and I say, "Janey, I just need five minutes. I need to sit quietly for five minutes, *alone*." And I go into my room and sit down and Janey follows, weeping. And we sit there and then she says, bitterly, "I wish that I were an older kid." And my rage instantly evaporates —

FRAN.   Uh huh

MOLLY.   And curiosity takes over —

FRAN.   Right.

MOLLY.   And I say, "Why do you wish you were an older kid?" and she says, "So that I could kill you."

FRAN.   Oh, god.

MOLLY.   And I say, "Right. You're so angry with me you wish that you could kill me." And then she says, "But — what, oh what will I do, for then I would miss you so much." And I say, "Right. *That's* the dilemma."

FRAN.   God. *(Pause.)* Molly. I think I'm going to have a baby.

MOLLY.   What?!

FRAN.   It looks good. She's due in a month. Seventeen years old. Knocked up by some guy she met in a restaurant where she works. Doesn't want to have the kid, wants to finish high school, have a life. Her parents are very supportive. I wrote her a letter about myself, about being a mother, and sent her snap shots of the apartment. It's so strange.

MOLLY.   Fran. This is so exciting.

FRAN.   Should I be doing this?

MOLLY.   I don't know.

FRAN. I'm so scared. I lie awake thinking, What if she changes her mind, what if she doesn't change her mind, what if it's a frog, what if it's a boy? I don't know anything about boys. What if it's a girl? Will I feel competitive? What will it look like? Will it be okay that it doesn't look like me? What if it's stupid? How conditional is my love? What if I don't know what I'm doing? And I hear you talk about what you're going through and I think, I'm not up to this. I don't know if I'm up to it.

MOLLY.   Oh, Fran. You know, you're going through the same stuff I did when I was pregnant with Janey.

FRAN.   *(Angry, controlled.)* No I'm not.

MOLLY.   *(Surprised.)* What?

FRAN.   You always do that.

MOLLY.   Do what?

FRAN.   You don't want to deal with my feelings.

MOLLY.   *(Completely thrown.)* What are you talking about?

FRAN.   You want to neutralize them, turn them into what everybody else feels.

MOLLY.   No I don't.

FRAN.   You do to. You do it all the time.

MOLLY.   Name one instance.

FRAN.   Easy. *(Beat. Suddenly very hard.)* When I told you my mother was dying. You said no she wasn't. *(Beat.)*

MOLLY.   *(Trying to reconstruct it.)* I couldn't bear it.

FRAN.   It was *my* mother. *(Beat.)*

MOLLY.   I didn't want it to be true. I didn't want you to be sad.

FRAN.   I wasn't sad. I was relieved.

MOLLY.   You were a wreck.

FRAN.   So don't I get to be?

MOLLY.   *(Beat, trying to sort her way through.)* I'm sorry. *(Beat.)* I felt you wanted me to take the rap for your mother's death.

FRAN.   *(Beat.)* I just wanted you there.

MOLLY.   You shut me out.

FRAN.   I had to. *(Confused silence.)*

MOLLY.   I'm sorry. *(Pause.)*

FRAN.   I've just been ... flooded with all these memories from my childhood, and this incredible longing for my parents.... Such a sadness that they're not here. Even though it was so awful, actually, they were so unhappy, were terrible parents, got married too young, he wasn't her class, always resented her.

MOLLY.   Uh huh.

FRAN.   And she was so bitter at the loss of her career, that she gave it up for him. She hadn't meant to. She still played in a local string quartet when we were young. I always felt her impatience with our interruptions, our tedious needs. And her desperation.

MOLLY.   She once told me you had great talent as a violinist. But that she'd wrecked it, had had too much wind in her sails.

FRAN.   *(Shocked.)* She *said* that?

MOLLY.   Uh huh.

FRAN.   I can't believe it.

MOLLY.   Why?

FRAN.   She might have said that to me.

MOLLY.   She probably figured you already knew it. You were there.

FRAN.   But ... it's so like her. She never spoke of it to me. *(Pause.)* I'm sorry.

MOLLY.   No, I'm sorry.

FRAN.   I have to go.

MOLLY.   Aren't you coming over for soup?

FRAN.   I can't.

MOLLY.   Fran, please.

FRAN.   I'm not good company.

MOLLY.   That's okay.

FRAN.   I'm sorry.

MOLLY.   Okay. Come say bye to Janey.

FRAN.   I can't.

MOLLY.   Franny.

FRAN.   I'll call you.

MOLLY.   Okay. *(Fran leaves, Molly watches her go.)*

End Scene

SCENE EIGHT

A room in a home for pregnant women. Jen is sitting there. She's seven months pregnant. Brena has just come in, is unloading her stuff, opening a tin of cookies.

BRENA.   Oh oh. I hope I didn't give that house lady one of the hash cookies. I was going to put some regular ones in ...

JEN.   *(Taking a cookie.)* Right.

BRENA.   I thought you needed a little fun in here. That lady was so uptight. I had to really lay it on thick, talk about Jesus and shit.

JEN.   God. She's gonna get really stoned.

BRENA.   She'll just think it's the flu.

JEN.   I can't believe they still let you out of the house.

BRENA.   Look who's talking. God. Melissa and I made a batch of these on the weekend, we were sitting around and she asked me something and, like, I started to answer but as soon as I get three words out, I'm, like, stranded, I can't remember the beginning of what I said or where I'm going. Like I was just sunk in the black hole, you know?

JEN.   They'll kill me if they ever find out. They're so uptight. Even if they see me with a candy bar or a can of soda — and forget coffee or booze. It's like a prison. It's like I feel like Hansel or Gretel or whoever it was the witch was fattening up for the roast except in the old days the witch just gave them food, she wasn't like into what's bad for you. I mean, they could care less what's bad for *me* — I mean they're like really nice to us in this really fake way but you know it's just because the bun is in the oven still, soon as they get their hands on it, we'll see if they remember us. *(Brena produces a bottle of Sprite from her bag. They pass the bottle back and forth during the following.)* Far out. *(Beat.)* We better hide this stuff before Marina comes back.

BRENA.   Who's she?

JEN.   She's eight months. She's only gained twenty pounds so she freaks out if she sees anything with calories because her boyfriend'll kill her if she comes back fat. She's got the adopting parents to give her an extra thou for relocation or psychological adjustment or something — her uncle's a lawyer so he made this great deal — so her and her boyfriend're going to Cancun.

BRENA.   Where's that?

JEN.   Some island in Tahiti or something. Anyway, she's kind of a pain in the ass because she cries a lot in the night and I can't sleep.

BRENA.   Can't you change rooms?

JEN.   *(Distracted, troubled.)* I don't know. *(Pause.)*

BRENA.   So. You coming back?

JEN.   I don't know.

BRENA.   I saw your mother the other day.

JEN.   Oh, yeah? How is the bitch?

BRENA.   Who knows.

JEN.   She's going through this whole fucking God trip on me. She writes me this letter full of all this flowery bull shit, "I won't abandon you in your distress, hate the sin but love the sinner, you are my child and will always be my child" but underneath clear as day is "You slut, you disgusting pig, how could you do something so dirty and disgusting, didn't I tell you not to let those pricks into your pants?!"

BRENA.   Yeah ...

JEN.   But she'd never let me come back with the baby, god, that would be too terrible to have this daily reminder of what a whore her daughter is and for all of her friends and neighbors to know — it's just too, too disgusting. *(They're high, each thinking her own private thoughts.)*

BRENA.   Yeah.

JEN.   I always feel like two people, you know?

BRENA.   *(Shakes head.)* Uh-uh.

JEN.   The person who had these feelings, these secret feelings and it's about feeling good, you know, from when you're little and you get that people don't like to see you rubbing yourself up against stuff to feel good, know what I mean?

BRENA. You're bad. *(They laugh.)*
JEN. So you like go underground ...
BRENA. You better!
JEN. And then when a guy kisses you or feels your tit or says something in your ear and you feel really hot and silky ... and on top of it, really intense, riding a wave. And ... it's so far from your life, the rest of your regular life. And it's fabulous. And it has nothing to do with, like, sex education —
BRENA. Huh?
JEN. Like everybody says, you asshole, why didn't you use anything —
BRENA. Who said that?
JEN. Anyway, everybody's thinking it. And they talk about how it makes *guys* feel ...
BRENA. Uh huh.
JEN. Like *they* have this, like, urge, these strong feelings but nobody wants to like admit — like they're scared or something that girls have these really hot feelings —
BRENA. *(Sarcastic.)* They don't.
JEN. So all they talk about is it's up to the girls to not let the guys into their pants —
BRENA. That's right.
JEN. And don't get pregnant and watch out for diseases and getting raped and, shit, I know there are a lot of assholes out there and I don't want to get diseased or raped but — shit.
BRENA. Yeah. *(Pause.)*
JEN. *(Putting her hand on her stomach.)* Hey, hey, hey!
BRENA. What?
JEN. She's kicking me. *(To stomach.)* Don't you listen to this, baby. God. She sure is lively.
BRENA. How come you call it a she?
JEN. 'Cause they did an amnio.
BRENA. What's that?
JEN. It's when the adopters want to know if it's going to be a boy or a girl. It's a girl.
BRENA. Wow. Cool. *(Pause.)*
JEN. I got a letter from the lady that wants to adopt her.

BRENA. Wow.

JEN. She lives in New York City. She isn't married. I thought that'd be good 'cause I'm not married. And the kid wouldn't grow up with a lot of arguing and stuff.

BRENA. Right.

JEN. She has some kind of job that she does in an office but she can do it at home if she wants.

BRENA. Wow.

JEN. Editing.

BRENA. Huh.

JEN. She lives in an apartment and she also has a house in the countryside in Massachusetts that she goes to sometimes on weekends and summer vacation. She has a garden.

BRENA. Wow.

JEN. I wonder what you have to do to get to be an editor.

BRENA. Yeah. *(Jen pulls out a letter, reads.)*

JEN. She says she's thirty-eight years old.

BRENA. Wow.

JEN. And she thinks that's good because she had a lot of time to get to know what she wanted to do in her life and have fun.

BRENA. Huh.

JEN. She says, "There's nothing I can think of that would be as gratifying as to bring up a child. To nurture and guide and teach and love."

BRENA. Huh.

JEN. Sounds good.

BRENA. Yeah. *(Pause.)*

JEN. I had this thought. That I could write her and say, okay, you can have the baby if you take me too.

BRENA. She's not going to want you.

JEN. I know, but maybe.

BRENA. No way.

JEN. She sounds so nice.

BRENA. She wants your baby.

JEN. Yeah. Or I was thinking I could just go to New York and find them.

BRENA. How're you going to find them? You got her address?

JEN.   No. They don't let you know that stuff. But, like, I could just look in all the playgrounds.

BRENA.   They don't have playgrounds in New York.

JEN.   They don't?

BRENA.   No way.

JEN.   Why would I want my kid to grow up in New York then?

BRENA.   *(Excited.)* Oh — god — Jason went to New York. He just split.

JEN.   *(Excited.)* I read about it in the Digest. What happened?

BRENA.   He found out Marcie's baby was really from Tom.

JEN.   She should've told him.

BRENA.   She was too scared.

JEN.   Did he start drinking again?

BRENA.   Not yet. And Chester stole Benny back.

JEN.   Oh my god.

BRENA.   And he doesn't have his medicine.

JEN.   God. What happened to Babs?

BRENA.   She's left Howie. She found out he was sleeping with Bernice. But he doesn't know she knows. And she and Rick are back together.

JEN.   Wow. *(Pause.)* I really dig Rick.

BRENA.   Yeah. *(Pause.)*

JEN.   It's weird. Like, sometimes I think about Frankie, like, what if he knew about it, what would he do, and what if he comes through the restaurant again and I'm there. I mean, maybe she's gonna look like him or something.

BRENA.   Yeah.

JEN.   Then I think, what if I could get a hold of him and maybe he'd lend me some money, just to get me started, just 'cause maybe he wouldn't want to give away his kid or something.

BRENA.   Yeah.

JEN.   It would just be so cool to have a baby and, like, you'd never feel alone anymore and if you ever needed a reason to, like, work hard or if you just felt, what's the point, just look over at her and that's it.

BRENA.   I don't know.

JEN.   But I don't even know his last name. I'm such a fool. *(Pause.)* You never saw him again after that night, did you?

BRENA.   Uh uh.

JEN.   *(To stomach.)* Hey, hey, easy does it. We're talking about your daddy, the fuck. *(They laugh.)* No — not really. I'll always say he was a cool guy, like, you don't want to grow up thinking your daddy was a shit.

BRENA.   Right.

JEN.   I'll just say he lost my number or something.

BRENA.   Yeah.

End Scene

SCENE NINE

Night. Molly and Fran standing arm in arm at a bus stop.

FRAN.   His father had a furniture shop. They fixed antique furniture. And he'd have the truck and we'd go there at night and sit in the dark with all the furniture. We'd smoke Camels and he'd tell me about Plato and Aristotle and then we'd drink Grand Marnier and neck.

MOLLY.   *(Laughs.)* Oh, god.

FRAN.   I remember one night he touched my breasts and I stopped him and he said, why, and I wasn't sure. I had to think about it. It wasn't — natural — for me. Being raised a Catholic this was all a sin so I was pretty tense, pretty cut off. But I liked the idea, you know, of romance and intimacy and disobedience.

MOLLY.   Right.

FRAN.   I remember sitting in the dark in this big room full of beds and up-ended chairs, making out their outlines in the dim light, trying to work out what I thought about him feeling my breasts, whether it was okay, whether I really thought it was a sin. I decided I didn't think it was a sin so we did it. It was very strange — I felt very outside it at first, but after a while I began to enjoy it. One night I remember getting really, you know, aroused —

MOLLY. Uh huh.

FRAN. And getting on top of him and pressing myself against him. Later, he told me that was the one time he didn't like. It seemed too forward or gross or something. So I stopped seeing him, just avoided him, never told him why. Until a couple of years later and we'd both had others, we each lost that precious virginity —

MOLLY. Uh huh.

FRAN. We met at a party and ended up at the shop and made it on one of the beds. I guess we were each proving something to the other. I guess he was showing me he now knew what to do and wasn't scared of it which I now realize was the problem but at the time, of course, I just felt so completely humiliated and — and that I shouldn't trust, you know, these feelings —

MOLLY. Uh huh.

FRAN. And I guess I was just — this sounds absurd — just being polite. I pretended I was, you know, into it —

MOLLY. Uh huh.

FRAN. But I kept remembering that one night and how it had turned him off. That was it. We never saw each other after that night. But that's how I got pregnant. I was eighteen. And ... Daddy knew a doctor. And it was taken care of.

MOLLY. Huh.

End Scene

SCENE TEN

Hospital room. Jen in bed wearing hospital gown. Sylvia sitting in a chair next to the bed.

JEN.   I want to see the baby. I just want to see the baby.

SYLVIA.   I know, dear. I know.

JEN.   Where are my clothes?

SYLVIA.   Your parents have them. They'll be here soon.

JEN.   You stole my clothes.

SYLVIA.   You'll get them back.

JEN.   I want to see the baby.

SYLVIA.   I know. *(Jen's father, Eugene, comes in. He has flowers.)*

EUGENE.   Hi, Jen.

JEN.   Hi, Daddy.

EUGENE.   Okay?

JEN.   Yeah. *(Sylvia begins to leave.)*

SYLVIA.   I'll find a vase.

EUGENE.   We'll take them home.

SYLVIA.   *(Flustered.)* Okay. I'll just ... *(Sylvia leaves.)*

EUGENE.   I brought you something. *(He gives her a toy stuffed animal.)*

JEN.   Thanks.

EUGENE.   For your collection. And here's some clothes your mother packed. *(Hands bag to Jen who takes it behind a curtain and dresses.)* She's feeling sick. Says she'll see you when you get home. *(Beat.)* We cleaned up your room, got it all ready for you. But I wouldn't let her take down the posters, said that was up to you. Your Uncle Harold and Aunt Grace are coming over for dinner. They want to see you. *(Sylvia comes in, goes behind curtain to check on Jen.)*

SYLVIA.   Mr. Sullivan is here. *(Mac comes in.)*

MAC.   Don't let me interrupt the family reunion. *(Jen comes out, Sylvia leaves.)* Hello, dear. They tell me you were a real trooper.

JEN.   They put me to sleep.

MAC.   Uh huh.

JEN.   I wanted to be awake. I wanted to see the baby.

MAC.   *(Smiles at Eugene.)* She wanted to be awake. *(To Jen.)* Believe me, there's nothing romantic about this event. Ask my wife. *(To both.)* The first kid she tried natural — after that, with the other two, they knocked her out. She said, please, we don't go through enough, we have to go through that hell as well? She said she got to hating men so bad during that first birth she thought the whole thing — procreation! — was a plot against women! She went crazy — almost turned her into a lesbian. Luckily, by the time I saw her she'd pretty much recovered. So you're glad the doctor took pity on you *(To Eugene.)* — right?

EUGENE.   That's right. *(Mac pulls out some papers, takes them to Jen.)*

MAC.   *(To Jen.)* Anyway, you'll have many more opportunities if you really want to go through it. You'll finish school, meet the right guy, settle down — you've got another chance for that ideal life — a lot of girls don't get that. Now, honey, just sign here. Just a formality. *(Jen looks at the papers, blurred by tears. Can't move.)* Come on, honey. It'll all seem like ancient history tomorrow.

JEN.   *(To Eugene.)* Do I have to?

EUGENE.   That's right. *(Jen signs the papers.)*

MAC.   *(Relieved.)* Good girl. *(Mac brings the papers to Eugene. He signs.)* Good. Now. Fine. All set. Okay, Jenny, you come along with me. Just a legality. We need to bring the package together into the lobby. *(To Eugene.)* Why don't you come along? *(They all go out.)*

End Scene

SCENE ELEVEN

Hospital lobby. Fran and Sylvia stand, waiting, across the lobby from a band of elevators.

SYLVIA.   I'll take the money.
FRAN.   Oh. Right. I'm sorry. Um. *(Fran fishes in her bag, pulls out an envelope, surreptitiously hands it to Sylvia who opens it and without pulling the money out, counts it, and puts it in her purse.)* I feel sick.
SYLVIA.   It's all right. It'll be okay.
FRAN.   Why is it taking so long?
SYLVIA.   It isn't taking so long.
FRAN.   Our flight leaves in an hour.
SYLVIA.   It's twenty minutes to the airport. You'll have plenty of time. Mr. Sullivan knows what he's doing.
FRAN.   What if she's changed her mind?
SYLVIA.   There's always another baby.
FRAN.   Fuck. She's changed her mind, hasn't she?
SYLVIA.   No. Believe me, she has no alternative.
FRAN.   *(Thrown.)* What do you mean?
SYLVIA.   She's a kid. What's she going to do? How's she going to take care of a baby? Her parents aren't going to help.
FRAN.   Oh, god.
SYLVIA.   Believe me, justice will prevail, thank God.
FRAN.   What?
SYLVIA.   You get a baby, the baby gets a mother, and the mother gets her future served up on a silver plate. Understand? *(Pause.)*
FRAN.   Why can't I have a receipt?
SYLVIA.   For what?
FRAN.   The money I just gave you.
SYLVIA.   Don't panic.
FRAN.   I'm not. I'm just asking.
SYLVIA.   *(Working to maintain control.)* I know Mr. Sullivan made it real clear that if you got a receipt for every expense

38

in the operation, it's gonna jeapordize the operation, understand? There is absolutely nothing illegal in this exchange, okay? I'm a professional. I did my job. But when you go to court for the finalization, how's it gonna look if you got all these receipts and fees you paid all along the way? It's gonna look a lot more organized than it really was and that's gonna make the judge real uncomfortable. If you want to do that, then fine.

FRAN. *(Trying to drop it.)* Okay.

SYLVIA. I'll say one thing: if my daughter'd been such a fool I'd'a knocked her upside the head.

FRAN. I'm sorry?

SYLVIA. I'm talking hanging on to what you got or you're just handing over your life for them to trash and burn.

FRAN. Yes.

SYLVIA. You gotta give these children the tools to survive, understand? I'd be on my daughter every day, year after year and she's at a great university now, you hear me? I'd kill for that child. *(The elevator door opens, out come Eugene arm in arm with Jen, and Mac holding the baby. Mac turns to Jen and Eugene, says good bye, sees Fran and Sylvia and walks quickly over to them. Jen and Eugene stand there watching.)*

MAC. *(Angry, under his breath.)* I told you to wait in the car. *(Fran is completely flustered, aware of the baby and of Jen across the lobby.)*

FRAN. Oh ... I thought ...

MAC. Let's go. Don't stop. *(Mac starts out the door with the baby. Fran and Jen are frozen, looking at each other. Mac comes back, takes Fran's arm, escorts her out. Hisses.)* Goddamnit, you want to wreck the whole thing, for Christsake let's get the fuck out of here. *(Fran glances back at Jen as Mac escorts her out. They're gone. Then Jen looks blankly at Sylvia who waves, embarrassed, and leaves. Jen weeps in Eugene's arms.)*

End Scene

SCENE TWELVE

Washington Square playground. Fran sits on the bench with Grace. There are two strollers, each with a sleeping child.

GRACE.   My father, he had a bakery. My mother had a shop. In the morning, my sisters, they would comb my hair. We would have breakfast, an egg and bread and Ovaltine. Or some days, oat porridge. My sister, she always had a cup of coffee, from the time she was two years old, she always liked it and my father, he let her have it. *(Pause. they watch the children.)* My mother, she had a car so sometime she drop us to school. On the way home we would be by my grandmother. She was the first house on the road home, so that's where we would go. *(Pause.)* For supper we would have rice with beans and vegetables, sometimes meat. Goat meat sometimes. Junji, a kind of corn meal. Eggplant. We like it spicy. Some days, you would hear the horn blowing and you would go down and get your fish. On Saturdays you would go down and get your meat. My father, his favorite thing was Campbells vegetable soup. He would put that on everything. *(Pause.)* My sisters, they came here first. They say there are more opportunities here and they can make out better. *(Pause.)* When I come here, the most surprising thing is that in the winter the sun is shining. I thought it would snow all the time. But that it could be cold and the sun shining I never thought could be. And the tall buildings, I never saw this. And the subway. And the way you have to be locked in, you know, locking the windows and locking the doors. And ... all the planning. You always have to be planning here. Back there you could just pass and drop in. You don't have to call. *(Pause.)* My baby, Carl, he is five. Daslele is eight. Junior is nine. They stay with my mother. And my sister, too, is there. When I first came I'd be thinking it's three o'clock, four o'clock, five o'clock, oh, they're home now, maybe now they're doing their homework, maybe now they're having their supper, now they should be in bed. I call twice a month. They complain to me. They tell me what they want. I send Daslele a cabbage patch doll with corn silk hair. And some Jordash jeans. Junior I send a little computer game and a camera. Carl, he only want money. *(Pause.)* I never wanted nobody to take care of me. Because then you can't say what's on your mind. Or if they don't like it then they stop taking care of you. So if they say jump, you jump. Now, if you say jump, I sit. *(Molly comes in, flops down between the women on the bench.)*

MOLLY.   Hi!

FRAN.   Molly! You made it!

MOLLY.   I have exactly forty two minutes before I have to be back. She's asleep! I can't believe it. *(Grabbing stroller, pretending anger.)* Carly! I'm here. I've got forty-two minutes of quality time and my baby is copping z's?!

FRAN.   We tried to keep her up, gave her coffee, dexidrine, nothing seemed to work.

MOLLY.   *(Resigned, pulling sandwich and drink out of paper bag.)* Oh, well. It's a fabulous day. It's great just to get out of there. How you doing, Grace? Everything went okay today?

GRACE.   She wanted to stay with Janey at school.

MOLLY.   Oh, dear.

GRACE.   But after that she was fine.

MOLLY.   How was the birthday party?

FRAN.   Great. Except your daughter kept on grabbing all of Tara's presents. I finally had to promise her that you'd bring home lots of presents for her tonight.

MOLLY.   Fran!

FRAN.   It was my last recourse.

GRACE.   *(Beginning to gather her things.)* Maybe I'll do those errands now, while you're here.

MOLLY.   Great.

FRAN.   *(To Molly.)* You look quite smashing.

MOLLY.   Do I? The proper tension between funky and chic? Makes you want to hand over all your loot to the Children's Art Fund?

FRAN.   Absolutely.

MOLLY.   Thanks, pal.

GRACE. I'll be back.
MOLLY. Okay.
FRAN. See you soon.
GRACE. All right. *(Grace leaves.)*
MOLLY. Look at them. They're such grown ups.
FRAN. Aren't they?
MOLLY. I can't stand it. How do people stand it?
FRAN. I don't know.
MOLLY. I mean, you work. You've always worked.
FRAN. It is easier, to work at home. To take breaks, have lunch with Tara. Knock off early. Work at night. That flexibility. And Mrs. Schmidman is great. And I do, often, actually enjoy my work. Of course, it is exhausting. I'm exhausted all the time.
MOLLY. If I could just get back the afternoons, going with Carly to pick up Janey from school, walking through the park, actually having a sense, over the months, of the seasons changing.
FRAN. Yes.
MOLLY. Stopping to examine a stone, a leaf, a piece of glass, an old condom ... *(They laugh.)*
FRAN. Ah, exotic nature!
MOLLY. Going to the market, visiting with Myung and Sun Jung, examining vegetables, imagining what I might cook. They'd give the girls Gummy Bears ...
FRAN. Mmm.
MOLLY. Stopping at Frankie's, practicing our Spanish, fighting over whether they can have more candy, dragging them, screaming, out of the store.
FRAN. Sounds delightful.
MOLLY. Going home, they'd play, or watch Sesame Street, or help me. Sometimes some little personal thought or question or event of the day would pop out ...
FRAN. Uh huh.
MOLLY. And I'd scrub the potatoes, scrape the carrots, chop the broccoli. Mundane tasks I never really thought about. But there's something nice about having that ... the smell and texture and color and shape of this stuff from the

earth ...

FRAN.   Huh.

MOLLY.   Now, I come home, they've had supper, the day's over. They seem fine. But ... I feel so distant. I pretend to connect. The other night, I was giving them a bath, they were arguing, complaining about something, I just lost it, screamed at them to shut up, stormed out, leaving them crying, hysterical. It was awful.

FRAN.   You were always bad around bath time.

MOLLY.   I was?

FRAN.   Yes.

MOLLY.   *(Thoughtful.)* I guess that's true. Maybe, if I had a snack before ... I get them tucked in, and if we have enough cash Jack and I order Chinese. Otherwise we have beer and granola for supper.

FRAN.   That's really pathetic.

MOLLY.   Isn't it?

FRAN.   I have a confession to make.

MOLLY.   Oh-oh.

FRAN.   Tara and I mainly eat in coffee shops. When I cook it's fish sticks or chicken pot pies.

MOLLY.   I did know that about you.

FRAN.   Oh. I suppose you did. We like it like that. *(Pause.)*

MOLLY.   If we can just catch up on our taxes, I could go back to part time. If I could start selling my paintings. If I could ever get back into the studio. If I ever paint again. *(Pause.)*

FRAN.   I've been thinking about the mother all day.

MOLLY.   You mean...?

FRAN.   Wondering if she remembers it's Tara's birthday, whether she thinks about her, what her life is like. I don't correspond with her. I gather she has the pictures I sent to her through the lawyer. Sometimes I want to talk with her, be with her. Other times I feel so threatened ... just that she's out there. *(Pause.)* I wonder whether she'll be in Tara's life when she's older.... Of course I won't keep the information from Tara, I'll dutifully follow the current thinking on letting the child know her history. *(Beat.)* I dreamed we were all together — she and Tara and I — on some rocks, a coast somewhere, very windy, wet. That's all I remember. *(Pause.)*

MOLLY.   She's your daughter, you know.

FRAN.   I know. Mine. The toddler's possessive.

MOLLY.   Sorry?

FRAN.   A clue on a recent crossword puzzle.

MOLLY.   Oh. *(Pause.)*

FRAN.   I've started to play the violin again.

MOLLY.   That's wonderful.

FRAN.   Yes, like returning to an old friend. And to be inside these pieces of music I'd banished myself from for so many years ... I tried to bring myself to play for my mother before she died. She'd be lying in bed, wasting away, becoming less, less of what she'd been, vaguer, sweeter. Or ... it was easier to project onto her. Or ... I had less need to project onto her. I remember, when we were driving her especially crazy, she'd tell us we were killing her and she'd lock herself up in the bathroom and we'd be hysterical, weeping, banging on the door, begging her to come out, not to die, we'd be good. I'd run and get my fiddle, play everything I knew, she'd eventually come out.

MOLLY.   Oh, Fran. *(Beat.)*

FRAN.   Once she told me how when Mozart was seventeen his father scolded him, told him he could be a great violinist if only he'd practice. He wrote six concerti between the ages of seventeen and nineteen. So the concerti were his way of malingering. He was avoiding practicing. *(Beat. Fran watches Tara.)* God, I adore her. *(Beat.)* I've composed a couple of songs for her. I can't get them out of my head.

MOLLY.   Fran! How wonderful! What are they?

FRAN.   The first is so she's inspired to drink her milk.

MOLLY.   *(Delighted.)* Oh.

FRAN.   *(Sings.)* "Milk, milk, milk, it comes from the cow or the goat. It goes right down your throat to your tummy! And we love a dove a dove a dove a dove it! Oh, the farmer goes to the cow and he says 'Thank you, cow, 'cause you know how to make milk, and we love a dove a dove a dove a dove it.' And the farmer pulls the teats of the cow and milk spurts into the bucket. And he takes the bucket of milk and pours it into some cartons. And he puts the cartons of milk on his truck and drives into the city and he sells the milk to the people in the store — you know what for — what for? For milk, milk, milk, it comes from the cow or the goat. It goes right down your throat to your tummy. And we love a dove a dove a dove a dove it."

MOLLY.   *(Watching the sleeping girls, happy.)* God, look at them. They're such angels. *(Checks her watch.)* I don't want to go back.

FRAN.   And the other is so Tara will sit on the potty and poop.

MOLLY.   Oh. How handy.

FRAN.   *(Sings.)* "Oh, poop-a-doop-a-doop, oh, poop-a doop-a-doop, how I love to poop. Oh, poop-a-doop-a-doop, oh, poop-a-doop-a-doop, how I love to poop. Well, there was a boy, he was sitting on the bus, and he had to poop. And he said to the bus driver, sir, what should I do..."

End Play

PROPERTY LIST

Coat (FRAN)
Plate of sushi (FRAN)
Book, *War and Peace* (JACK)
Dog magazine (ELLIE)
Cup of ice chips (ELLIE)
Baby (MOLLY)
Tea (JACK, FRAN)
Baby in Snuglie (MOLLY)
Cookie tin with cookies (BRENA)
Bottle of Sprite (BRENA)
Letters (JEN)
Flowers (EUGENE)
Stuffed animal toy (EUGENE)
Bag with clothes for Jen (EUGENE)
Papers for signing (MAC)
Bag (FRAN)
Envelope with money (FRAN)
Purse (SYLVIA)
2 strollers
Paper bag with sandwich and drink (MOLLY)